KT-431-919

Books should be returned or renewed by the
last date stamped above

362.50942

EAL Telling Our Stories

Public Record Office
Pocket Guides to Family History

USING

POOR LAW RECORDS

Simon Fowler

PUBLIC RECORD OFFICE

ISBN 1 903365 07 4

A catalogue card for this book
is available from the British Library

Front cover: 'Remember the sweeper!'
Spurgeon Collection (no. 26)
Photograph by R.L. Sims of Greenwich
Registered for copyright by
Charles Spurgeon 24 September 1884
Reproduced by courtesy of
Greenwich Local History Library,
London Borough of Greenwich
(COPY 1/369)

Printed by Cromwell Press, Trowbridge, Wiltshire

CONTENTS

INTRODUCTION

Poor Law records are a valuable source for family history. They contain much of interest about people who might otherwise have totally disappeared from the written record. Although they can be difficult to track down and use, if you think you had an ancestor who was poor it is worth persevering.

This *Pocket Guide* shows you how to find and use this material. It describes both the Old and the New Poor Laws over a period of nearly 350 years, between 1601 and 1948. It also explains where to start with the records of charities, which may help you to locate a poor ancestor.

There was a complete break in administration of the poor in 1834. Prior to that date, under the Old Poor Law, poor people were looked after by the parishes in which they lived or were born (not necessarily the same thing). After the New Poor Law was introduced in 1834, paupers were to be kept in workhouses administered by a group of parishes, known as a Poor Law union. There was also increased supervision of this work by Whitehall.

Most Poor Law records are at local record offices, because care of the poor was very much a local responsibility. The Public Record Office (PRO), however, has correspondence with Poor Law unions between 1834 and 1900, registers of people who worked in workhouses and a set of Parliamentary Papers, which may contain references to individuals.

WAS MY ANCESTOR POOR?

Being poor has always had a certain stigma attached to it. It is not something to which people like to admit. It is possible, however, that there are family stories about being admitted to the workhouse; or, very occasionally, settlement certificates and related documents may turn up in family papers.

You may also find clues while researching your family history in archives. Many people become aware of poverty in their family only when they turn up an entry in a parish register indicating that an ancestor was a pauper (the universal term for anybody in receipt of any assistance from the parish). It might also be worth checking if you have ancestors who lived to a great age, say, over sixty, for they may well have received a small pension, often called 'out-relief', from the authorities. There are also likely to be records about single mothers and their children. In addition, between about 1810 and 1834, labourers and their families living in southern rural parishes may well have received some support as well. At any one time, up to 20 per cent of the population of some villages may have been on poor relief.

You may be able to identify paupers from descriptions on birth and death certificates and entries in census enumerators' books. Death certificates will also note whether a person died in the workhouse. If a person was very old when he or she died and came from a poor background, it is quite likely that she or he was admitted to the workhouse, particularly in the decades after 1850. Similarly many single mothers gave birth to illegitimate children in the workhouse, as this was one of the few places that admitted 'fallen' women and their babies.

Family Records Centre

The Family Records Centre (FRC) in Clerkenwell, London, has records which might help track down an ancestor who was in receipt of poor relief.

The FRC is a service for family historians, set up in 1997 by the Office for National Statistics (ONS) and the Public Record Office. It provides a comprehensive reference resource including indexes to the major sources for family history in the United Kingdom, microfilm copies of a wide range of documents, including birth, marriage and death records and the census for England and Wales, CD-ROMs, online search facilities, and a large collection of reference books, indexes and maps. No original documents are kept at the FRC. If you need to see original material, you will need to go to the PRO at Kew.

▼ **Family Records Centre**
  1 Myddleton Street
  London EC1R 1UW
  Telephone: 020 8392 5300
  Fax: 020 8392 5307
  Internet: http://www.pro.gov.uk/frc/

You can visit the FRC in person without an appointment. If you are disabled and require parking, phone first. There are some disabled parking spaces, but they need to be booked in advance.

Opening times (closed Sundays and public holidays):

Monday	9 a.m. to 5 p.m.
Tuesday	10 a.m. to 7 p.m.
Wednesday	9 a.m. to 5 p.m.
Thursday	9 a.m. to 7 p.m.
Friday	9 a.m. to 5 p.m.
Saturday	9.30 a.m. to 5 p.m.

Birth, marriage and death records after 1 July 1837

These records, on the ground floor of the FRC, are for only England and Wales. Where no father is indicated on the birth certificate, the birth was illegitimate. Illegitimacy rates declined during the nineteenth century from a high of about seven per cent in the 1850s to four per cent in the 1890s. Many illegitimate births took place in workhouse infirmaries, and it is worth checking workhouse registers of births (if they survive) at the appropriate local record office to see whether the birth you are interested in appears there. If the place of birth is indicated as 'union workhouse' or something similar, again, it is worth seeing whether the workhouse register survives.

Many elderly and infirm people without a family to support them were admitted to the workhouse, particularly during the last part of the nineteenth century, when they were the largest group of residents. If the workhouse is indicated as the place of death, or the workhouse master or matron is the person who reported the event, it is worth seeing whether there are registers of admission or death for the particular workhouse at the appropriate local record office.

For more about certificates, see PRO, *Using Birth, Marriage and Death Records*.

Census

The earliest census of use to family historians is the 1841 census. The latest one available is that for 1891. The 1901 census will be opened on 2 January 2002. Census records can be consulted on the first floor at the FRC.

Census records are arranged by enumeration district within towns or rural districts. It can thus be difficult to track down an individual. Fortunately, help is at hand in the shape of surname and street indexes. There are name indexes for the whole of the 1881 census, most of 1851, and parts of the other censuses. The 1881 census index is on CD-ROM and is readily available at libraries around the country. A surname index for the whole of the 1901 census will be made available when these records are released in January 2002. In addition, there are a number of street indexes to London and large towns and cities, which can make searching considerably easier if you know a street where an ancestor lived at about the time of the census.

It is often fairly easy to identify paupers in census returns. For people receiving out-relief, the entry in the occupations column may read something like 'pauper', 'on the parish' or 'on relief'. However, individuals noted as 'annuitants' are likely to have been in receipt of a private pension. In 1891 there were also additional columns in the census enumerators' books, indicating whether an individual was unemployed and also whether the household had four or more rooms. This may be an indicator of poverty within a family, although the instructions regarding filling in these columns were confusing, so people often put in the wrong information. Workhouse masters and other employees of Poor Law unions are also likely to be identified as such.

Workhouses, workhouse schools, county lunatic asylums, almshouses and the like appear in the census in the normal way. Sometimes the names of the occupants are listed, but it is more common (and more frustrating) just to find initials. This was a simple – and effective – way of guaranteeing anonymity to the inmates. Even so, it may sometimes be possible to identify a person if they had unusual initials and you know their age.

For more about census records, see PRO, *Using Census Records*.

WHERE TO GO TO SEARCH POOR LAW RECORDS

Local record offices

The Poor Law was a local responsibility until 1834, and was shared with the government after then. Local record offices are therefore usually the best place to begin to look for ancestors who were involved with the Poor Law, either as administrators or as recipients of aid.

Every county has a county record office: some larger cities, such as Southampton or Coventry, also have a city record office as well. These record offices hold both material created by local government, such as rate books, quarter session records and council minutes, and unofficial material donated by individuals, companies or clubs, including land and house deeds, account books and photographs. Their holdings of Poor Law union material are described in J. Gibson, *Poor Law Union Records*, while quarter sessions documents are covered in his *Quarter Sessions Records for Family Historians*.

I. Mortimer (ed.), *Record Repositories in Great Britain*, will give you the addresses of local record offices. This information is available on the website of the National Register of Archives (NRA), which also contains a database of the holdings of local record offices. The National Register of Archives has a public reading room where lists of records can be consulted. Their address is:

▼ **The National Register of Archives**
  Quality House
  Quality Court
  Chancery Lane
  London WC2A 1HP
  Telephone: 020 7242 1198
  Internet: http://www.hmc.gov

Many county record offices have restricted space for readers. It is essential that you ring in advance to book a seat and to confirm that they have the records you are interested in. The usual rules about using pencils and treating the documents with care also apply.

ⓘ **Remember**
Most records about individual paupers are in local record offices.

Public Record Office

The Public Record Office is the national archives of the United Kingdom – and England and Wales. The PRO has records created, or acquired, by central government and the central law courts over more than 900 years.

▼ **Public Record Office**
  Kew
  Richmond
  Surrey TW9 4DU

General telephone: 020 8876 3444
Telephone number for enquiries: 020 8392 5200
Internet: http://www.pro.gov.uk/

Opening times (closed Sundays and Bank Holidays)

Monday	9 a.m. to 5 p.m.
Tuesday	10 a.m. to 7 p.m.
Wednesday	9 a.m. to 5 p.m.
Thursday	9 a.m. to 7 p.m.
Friday	9 a.m. to 5 p.m.
Saturday	9.30 a.m. to 5 p.m.

No appointment is needed to visit the PRO in Kew, but you will need a reader's ticket to gain acces to the research areas. To obtain a ticket you need to take with you a full UK driving licence or a UK banker's card or a passport if you are a British citizen, and your passport or national identity card if you are not. Note that the last time for ordering documents is 4 p.m. on Mondays, Wednesdays and Fridays; 4.30 p.m. on Tuesdays and Thursdays, and 2.30 p.m. on Saturdays.

Records at the PRO are normally kept together according to the government department that created them. Departments are given prefixes called departmental codes. The Ministry of Health and its predecessors, for example, is MH; and the Foreign Office is FO. Within each department, similar types of records are kept together in series, or collections, of records, each of which is assigned a unique number. Thus the

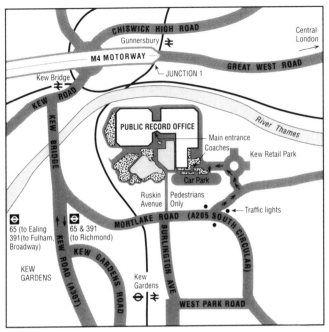

How to find the Public Record Office, Kew

series MH 12, for example, contains correspondence between the Poor Law Commissioners and their successors in Whitehall and local Poor Law unions; and MH 14 contains maps and plans for workhouses. Within each series, each piece – normally a file or volume – is given a unique reference. It is this three-part reference that you order, and quote in correspondence or books. For example, MH 14/65 is the reference for a file entitled 'Nottingham workhouse: sale of land, 1880–1915'.

What to take with you to the PRO

- £1 coin (refundable) so you can leave baggage in a locker

- money or a credit card if you are intending to buy copies of any records

- pencil (ink and rubbers are not allowed at Kew in case they damage original records, but they are allowed at the FRC)

- paper to record what you find (notebooks are allowed at both the FRC and Kew, but at Kew no more than six loose sheets are permitted)

- a record of any research you have done so far, to make sure you don't go through anything twice unnecessarily

- a laptop computer, if you wish

In the past you had to look up your references in catalogues, which listed every piece in each series. These catalogues are still available, but have largely been superseded by the electronic catalogue, which can be searched by subject. For example, you can now find nearly 3,000 references to 'charities' by typing this word into the computer. The electronic catalogue is also available on the PRO's website (http://www.pro.gov.uk).

ⓘ **Remember**
The PRO has no records about the working of the Poor Laws before 1834.

Local studies libraries

Local studies libraries are the poor relations of the archive world, mainly because they are neither an archive nor a library but contain elements of both. Their resources for family historians in general are described on the *Familia* website (http://www.earl.org.uk/familia). They are likely to have a comprehensive collection of books about the locality, including any on the Poor Law. For many users their greatest asset is a comprehensively indexed collection of press cuttings from local, and sometimes national, newspapers going back to before the First World War. Occasionally they may have original workhouse registers or other records. Normally this is noted in J. Gibson's *Poor Law Union Records*.

It can be difficult to locate local studies libraries. They are, however, normally part of a central reference library. Many are listed in Foster and Shepherd's *British Archives: A Guide to Archive Resources in the United Kingdom*.

Published sources

An increasing number of local family history and record societies are transcribing and publishing extracts from Poor Law records for their area. Copies of most family history society and many record society publications can be found in the library of the Society of Genealogists, 14 Charterhouse Buildings, Goswell Road, London EC1M 7BA (020 7251 8799). Their library catalogue can now be found on the Society's website (http://www.sog.org.uk). The PRO library has almost all record society publications.

THE OLD POOR LAW

Before 1834 the very poorest in society were cared for by the parish in which they lived or had right of settlement. During medieval times it had been the duty of the church to care for the poor as laid down in the scriptures. The abolition of the monasteries and the Reformation led to a succession of ineffectual and cruel laws. The Poor Law of 1547, for example, allowed branding and slavery as punishment for persistent vagrancy, and one of 1572 ordered beggars to be branded on the shoulder. Meanwhile private charity was left to cope with the elderly and the chronically sick, who were the people who most needed help.

Eventually Parliament took effective action with the 'Act for the Relief of the Poor' of 1601 – often called the '43rd Elizabeth', because it was passed in the 43rd year of Elizabeth I's reign. This legislation was the basis of the Old Poor Law until it crumbled under the great pressures unleashed by the Industrial Revolution. Each parish was to elect one or two substantial householders each year to be overseers of the poor, imposing on them the duty of maintaining the poor and setting them to work. The funds were to be provided by the levy of a poor rate on the inhabitants of the parish.

During the eighteenth century, and even more so during the early years of the nineteenth, many parishes established workhouses to house paupers. The intention was to reduce the cost of the poor rate by forcing all those in receipt of assistance to live together. Although conditions in workhouses were meant to deter people from claiming poor relief, many parishes took great pride in maintaining a welcoming home for their elderly and infirm. These were the precursors of the workhouses that were to become the centre of the later Victorian Poor Law.

Not every parish established a workhouse, and in many places the poor, especially the elderly and infirm, were well treated. As each parish took care of its own, however, the quality of assistance offered could vary tremendously. In part this might depend on local circumstance. A prosperous rural parish might have very few elderly or paupers to look after, while in towns there might be dozens, or even hundreds, of the poor seeking assistance. Another factor was the interest shown by the overseers in their work. It was a thankless and unpaid duty in which few men outside the clergy had any special interest. The overseers were often local farmers (in rural parishes) and shopkeepers and merchants (in the towns), who naturally wanted to keep expenditure as low as possible.

A lot also depended on the quality of any officials paid to run the workhouse or pay out pensions to widows. Their experience and ability varied greatly, and this would have had an impact on the provision made for the poor. Richmond, in Surrey, with its affluent population of concerned citizens, long had a reputation for the efficient administration of the Poor Law. Across the Thames in Brentford, however, the position was very different. Here the poor relief was renowned for its corruption and inefficiency, for the same family ran the local workhouse for many years.

The Poor Law system worked reasonably well in the stable, largely agrarian, society that was England during the seventeenth and eighteenth centuries. By the 1790s the population was beginning to rise rapidly, however, and the Industrial Revolution was beginning to attract people to the new industrial towns of the north.

Rural areas were particularly affected, as new methods of farming put thousands of agricultural labourers out of work. A solution adopted in many places was to use the poor rate to make up labourers' wages. The first parish to do so was Speenhamland, in Berkshire, in 1795, where the overseers of the poor agreed to supplement low wages with an allowance paid from the rates. This 'Speenhamland System' was widely adopted across southern England. An alternative was to assign unemployed labourers to local farmers, whether they needed extra labour or not. Part of their wages was met by the parish, and part by the farmer himself.

Although adopted with the best intentions, these solutions to rural unemployment actually added to the problem. Because local farmers often deliberately kept wages low, in the expectation that allowances would be given by the parish, the number of people on poor relief actually rose. This imposed enormous strain on the system as more and more people sought relief for themselves and their families. The amount paid in poor relief rose from £2m in 1783 to £7m in 1820.

It became clear that the old system could no longer cope: it was making idle tens of thousands who would rather work and not directing assistance to where it was most needed. Middle class commentators also identified the growth of a class of people – paupers – who, they argued, would not work, but preferred instead a life of indolence on the poor rate and were largely responsible for the growth of expenditure on the poor.

A royal commission was appointed in February 1832 to investigate and make recommendations. It reported two years later, having undertaken a massive survey of the current position. It proposed a major overhaul of the Poor Law, establishing Poor Law unions made up of groups of parishes to run workhouses, where all paupers were to be housed.

OLD POOR LAW – THE RECORDS

The records described below are those most relevant to the period of the Old Poor Law, although some of them extend beyond 1834. They are mainly to be found at county record offices. Their survival is patchy, however, so it is a very good idea to contact the record office in advance before you set out.

(i) **Remember**
Records of the Old Poor Law end in 1824.

Parochial records

Each of the 15,000 or so parishes in England and Wales had to appoint overseers of the poor every year. The overseers themselves created many records, the most important of which are probably the accounts, which record what was spent by the overseers in the course of their duties. From the accounts one can get a pretty good idea of the scope of the overseers' work, which included paying pensions to widows and widowers, removing paupers to other parishes, and purchasing clothing for orphans and medicine for the elderly. Although sometimes difficult to read, these accounts are full of human detail and may well mention grants and pensions paid to your ancestors.

The overseers were responsible to the parish vestry, which discussed and approved the actions of their officers. Where they survive, vestry minutes may record why payments were made to pauper ancestors and the result of their actions.

Another important administrative body was the quarter sessions, the quarterly meeting of all the magistrates of the county. Paupers threatened with removal or unhappy with their treatment could appeal to the quarter sessions. The survival of quarter sessions records is very patchy. Cambridgeshire quarter sessions records, for example, are almost non-existent, whereas most survive for Surrey. They can be difficult to use, often being in Latin before 1733, and the judgements themselves can be hard to read. A simple introduction to these records is J. Gibson, *Quarter Sessions Records for Family Historians*. Lists of many quarter sessions records are now available on the internet as part of the Access to Archives (A2A) project, accessible through the PRO website (http://www.pro.gov.uk).

The sessions were particularly harsh on vagrants, rogues and vagabonds, who were perceived as a threat to the peace. For the most part, these people were men and women tramping the country seeking work. Vagrants were examined, and orders issued for removal to their place of settlement. The records can give you some idea of where they were heading, as well as their personal circumstances. As the numbers on the tramp increased dramatically after the Napoleonic Wars, the system gradually fell into disuse – which may explain why there is relatively little material after 1820.

Settlement

By far the most important series of records relates to the administration of the Law of Settlement, introduced in 1662. The law established the principle of the right of settlement, which was granted to people who were either born in a parish, or had rented property, paid the poor rate, been apprenticed for seven years, or lived for a period of ten years or more in their new parish of residence. If you could not prove your right of settlement when you sought help, you were liable to be sent back to the parish of your birth. Parishes spent considerable amounts of time and money seeking to remove paupers from their jurisdiction, often far more than the expense of actually maintaining the individual. As a result, a great deal of paperwork was created. As much as half the business at quarter sessions could consist of deciding appeals by paupers against removal to another parish.

In these cases claimants were examined by local magistrates, who sought to identify in which parish they had right of settlement. These records offer a vivid insight into eighteenth-century life and the lives of the very poorest in particular. The person seeking settlement would be keen to stress his or her history of employment, often citing individual masters or mistresses, as well as their place of birth and places in which they had lived. For men, details of wife and children are sometimes given. These examinations, if they survive, are normally found in the quarter sessions records.

Removal orders returning paupers to their parish of settlement are another useful source. These are usually also found in quarter sessions records. As two copies of the order were made for each parish involved, their survival rate is relatively good. Late eighteenth and early nineteenth century orders can be particularly informative, giving reasons for the person's removal and other details of a family's circumstances; for example, whether the father was in prison or a woman was pregnant.

ⓘ **Remember**
You can often track movements of the poor in surviving quarter sessions records by looking at appeals against removal to another parish. These records are in Latin before 1733.

Paupers were given certificates from their parish of settlement that guaranteed to receive them back if they sought assistance. The information given in these certificates varies, but can include details not just of an individual, but of his or her family as well. Like all Poor Law records, their survival is patchy; occasionally they may be part of a family's papers, but much more often they can be found in the parish papers relating to poor relief at county record offices.

Although settlement was not formally abolished until 1948, it gradually fell into disuse with the New Poor Law, especially after 1867 when payment of rates within each Poor Law union was equalised. This reduced the need to remove paupers between neighbouring parishes.

Bastardy

Parish authorities were also responsible for the maintenance of single mothers and their illegitimate children. Much time was spent seeking the father and making him either marry the unfortunate woman or assume responsibility for her maintenance. Until the first years of the nineteenth century, however, bastardy was a minor problem and illegitimacy rates rarely rose above 3 per cent.

Once an overseer of the poor knew who the father of an illegitimate child was, he would issue a bastardy bond, which was an agreement between the man and the parish to pay costs relating to the child. On the birth of the child a maintenance order was made in which the man was ordered to pay a named sum, being the costs of the birth plus a weekly amount for maintenance of the child. If a man accused of fathering a child tried to run away, the overseers would issue a bastardy warrant to track him down and force him to pay towards the upkeep of his child. The information contained in these records varies, depending on the circumstances and the diligence of local officials, but you should be able to find out about the father and his occupation and the date and place of birth of the child.

Even after 1834 the authorities still made considerable attempts to identify the fathers of illegitimate children and make them pay for the upkeep of these children. There may be material in the Poor Law union records, particularly the minutes of the boards of guardians. There may also be orders for maintenance under the Bastardy Act of 1845.

Apprenticeship

Poor children, especially those who were maintained by the parish, could be apprenticed to local traders and shopkeepers. This was one way of reducing the poor rate, as they became the responsibility of the master, but it was also hoped that they might learn a useful trade and not repeat the mistakes of their parents. The conditions under which the apprentices lived were often appalling, for their new masters might regard them as nothing but cheap labour.

Copies of pauper apprenticeship documents (or indentures) are often to be found in parish records. They give the name of the individual and the person to whom he or she was being apprenticed. The trade to be taught is often given. The apprenticing of individual children is usually recorded in the vestry minute books or the overseer's accounts.

ⓘ **Remember**
Pauper apprenticeships were exempt from tax and therefore not included in the apprenticeship tax records in the PRO series IR 1.

Although pauper children were still apprenticed out after 1834, much greater care was taken about who they were apprenticed to. Guardians often inspected the places where children were to be sent, and this may be recorded in the minutes of the boards of guardians. There may also be registers of apprentices and copies of indentures and other records.

THE NEW POOR LAW

Origin

During the first decades of the nineteenth century it was increasingly clear that the Old Poor Law could not cope with the rising number of paupers. The poor rate, which paid for their care, was an increasing burden on middle-class pockets. Spending on the Poor Law rose from about £4m in 1800 to £7m by 1830. This rise in pauperism was largely the result of dislocation caused by the Agricultural and Industrial Revolutions and the aftermath of the Napoleonic Wars. Rural and semi-rural areas were particularly badly affected.

This was coupled with a growing sentiment that the real enemy was not poverty but pauperism – a character defect involving idleness, unreliability and above all drunkenness, which threatened the stability and respectability of society.

In 1832 the government set up a royal commission to investigate the situation ('His Majesty's Commissioners for Inquiry into the Administration and Practical Operation of the Poor Laws'). Its report, which was largely enacted as the Poor Law (Amendment) Act 1834, had a simple solution to the problem. Outdoor relief was to be phased out. Everybody who applied for assistance would be offered accommodation in the workhouse. There, their lives would be regulated and made less comfortable than those of people who decided to stay outside and fend for themselves. Only those who were in dire need would accept the workhouse. The commission's report was flawed in that it over-estimated the problem of pauperism. Most able-bodied men who sought relief were the victims of unemployment or low wages rather than wastrels.

The new Act met with stiff resistance, particularly in the north, where considerable protests were mounted against the 'pauper's Bastille', as the protesters called the workhouses. The first Poor Law unions were formed in southern England during 1835, but it was not until 1837 and 1838 that unions began to appear in the industrial areas of the north. In a few places Poor Law unions were not established until the 1870s.

Organisation

The basic administrative units of the New Poor Law were the Poor Law unions, 643 of which were eventually created throughout England and Wales. These unions, which consisted of a group of parishes, were responsible for the implementation of the Poor Law locally. Unions might well include parishes from several different counties. Their boundaries might well change over time, particularly in large towns and cities. Full details of the composition of individual unions are given in J. Gibson's *Poor Law Union Records*.

Their work was directed by an elected board of guardians. These were elected annually by local rate-payers, although magistrates were ex-officio members. The guardians were a mixture of local gentry and small businessmen. One of the constant complaints made about the administration of unions was the penny-pinching way in which they carried out their work – which critics blamed on the number of shopkeepers on the board, who were determined to keep the rates down rather than improve conditions in the work-house. During the 1880s a small number of women, and from the 1890s working-class men, were elected as guardians. On the whole, these new faces brought a breath of welcome humanity and common sense to the workhouse.

The formal business of the guardians was discussed at the board meeting, normally held weekly. In smaller unions the board might discuss the admission and discharge of individual paupers and any punishment meted out to them. Over time, in most unions a system of committees grew up to oversee aspects of the work. These could include boarding-out (supervising children placed with local families), dispensary, finance, general-purpose, house (supervising the workhouse), stores and women's committees.

Each union maintained at least one workhouse. In addition there might be a school and an infirmary for inmates. Particularly in the London area, unions might cooperate to run a school or asylum.

The most important official was the workhouse master, often assisted by his wife as the workhouse matron. In the early years, at least, they often ran the house without help. In 1834, for example, the master and his wife at the Southwell workhouse looked after 158 paupers. Another important official was the relieving officer, responsible for admitting paupers to the workhouse. Unions also employed clerks to the guardians, treasurers, medical officers, schoolmasters and mistresses, and chaplains. In the smaller unions these people might well be local solicitors, general practitioners and clergymen, who would receive a small stipend in return for services rendered.

Unions received advice, and a modicum of direction, from Whitehall in the form of the Poor Law Commissioners (1834–47), Poor Law Board (1848–71), Local Government Board (1871–19) and Ministry of Health (1919–29). In addition a number of Poor Law inspectors (originally assistant Poor Law commissioners) constantly visited workhouses to ensure that a minimum standard was met, while district auditors combed the accounts in search of unauthorised or irregular expenditure. The reports of the inspectorate can be very illuminating about workhouses and the conditions of the poor locally, although names of individuals are very rarely to be found.

The Poor Law was financed by a rate levied on ratepayers. Before 1862 this was collected by individual parishes, but thereafter it was assessed and collected by the union. In an attempt to equalise the burden on ratepayers between the richer unions in the West End of London and the poorer ones in the East End, after 1865 the poor rate in London was collected by the Metropolitan Common Poor Fund and apportioned where the need was greatest.

The workhouse

The first workhouse opened in Bristol in 1698. The idea gradually spread, so that by the end of the Old Poor Law in 1834, most parishes had one or more work-houses, or 'houses of industry' as they were sometimes called. With the establishment of Poor Law unions, parochial workhouses were closed down. They were generally replaced by a purpose-built central insti-tution – 300 new workhouses were constructed in the decade after the establishment of Poor Law unions.

Certain principles were generally followed in the workhouse. Men and women were kept separate, and there was a further division between those who were thought capable of work (known as able-bodied paupers) and those who were not. Families were broken up and children, except babies, were taken from their mothers. People slept in dormitories (generally called wards). There was a workyard where paupers would earn their keep by breaking stones and picking oakum. The worst conditions were probably found in the casual wards, which housed vagrants tramping the country looking for work. In return for a few hours' hard labour, such people could spend the night and receive a bowl of gruel.

For most paupers and their masters, a matter of crucial importance was food and drink. Diet was laid down in Whitehall, although workhouses had a choice of six dietaries, allowing some local discretion. For example, the Poor Law Board recommended in 1869 that able-bodied paupers should have for breakfast seven ounces of bread and one and a half pints of porridge. The diet was filling but desperately dull. At Christmas and on national celebrations such as Queen Victoria's Diamond Jubilee, however, inmates were regularly treated to roast beef and perhaps a glass of beer.

The workhouses soon got the reputation, which still haunts them today, of being cruel and heartless places. During the 1840s, there were a number of scandals about conditions in workhouses that reinforced this view. The worst of these was at Andover. Conditions at the local workhouse were so bad during 1846 that the paupers were reduced to eating the marrow of the bones they were supposed to be crushing for fertilizer.

After the 1850s workhouses increasingly became the refuge of outcasts from society. Residents over-whelmingly consisted of the elderly, orphans, nursing mothers with illegitimate children, and the insane. The Royal Commission on the Aged Poor of 1897 found that a third of old people over the age of 70 were helped in some way by the Poor Law authorities. From about this time, conditions slowly began to improve. Particular attention was paid to the schooling of children in the home, in the hope that they would not follow their parents' example; and in many unions children were raised in cottage homes away from the regimented life of the workhouse. In small ways, too, life in the workhouse got better, especially for the elderly. Old couples were allowed to see each other during the day, and the diet improved.

Despite the Act of 1834 and circulars from Whitehall in 1841 and 1869, the old system of out-relief (that is, paying pensions to paupers outside the workhouse) continued. By the end of the century, three-quarters of all poor people were receiving out-relief. Guardians realised that it cost less and was more humane.

Despite these changes, by the beginning of the twentieth century the workhouse was increasingly seen as outdated. The government set up a royal commission in November 1905 to investigate the Poor Law and make recommendations for its reform. It proposed that Poor Law unions be abolished and their duties passed to local government. It was not until 1929, however, that this recommendation was put into practice, with the passing of the Local Government Act. Most workhouses became hospitals for the elderly; a few of these still remain in use, although they have now largely been demolished. Nevertheless, the Poor Law was not finally abolished until 1948, when the Welfare State was introduced.

NEW POOR LAW – THE RECORDS

Records of the New Poor Law are split between the PRO at Kew and local record offices. Material relating to the day-to-day operations of individual Poor Law unions are generally to be found locally, while the PRO has documents on relations with the Poor Law Commissioners and their successors. For this reason it may be difficult to find very much about individual paupers at Kew.

Public Record Office

Correspondence (MH 12)

The major source for the Poor Law at the PRO is the correspondence between the Poor Law Commissioners (and their successors) and individual unions, which can be found in the series MH 12. There are some 16,741 volumes of bound papers arranged by county and union. They begin in 1834 and finish about 1900. Most records after 1900 were destroyed in the Blitz; what little survives is in MH 68.

Many of the volumes are in a poor condition and very dirty, so they should be treated with care. If in doubt about how to handle this material, please seek the advice of staff.

The contents of each volume vary greatly. The greater part of each piece is made up of correspondence with

Whitehall, mainly about policy, but occasionally about individual paupers whose cases were unusual or bitterly contested elections to boards of guardians.

There is also considerable correspondence about the workhouse, particularly at times when building work was planned. You will often find reports from Poor Law inspectors on conditions they found in the workhouses they inspected. The commissioners in London also took particular interest in the diet of paupers. Any variation from an official dietary had to be approved by Whitehall, and this often led to a lively exchange of letters. This material can give a vivid idea of what it must have been like to have been a resident of the workhouse. There are also plans of lands and buildings in the series MH 14, listed alphabetically by union between 1861 and 1918.

Amongst this correspondence you will probably also find returns to circulars sent out by the commissioners. These include lists of people vaccinated against smallpox in the union, paupers granted money to emigrate, and details of pauper 'lunatics' and where they were looked after. MH 19/22 and MH 64 contain further material about pauper emigrants.

Scattered through the volumes are application forms from people seeking employment with the union – as workhouse master, teacher or medical officer. These forms were introduced in 1842 for medical officers, but were extended in the mid-1840s to other staff. The forms give the full name of an individual, his age, previous jobs and reasons for appointment, together with the salary to be paid. In addition, name of wife and number of children, religion of the applicant and details of qualifications are sometimes given. There may also be letters from employees complaining about conditions or seeking pay rises.

During the 1870s unions, particularly in rural areas, took on responsibility for sanitation and slum clearance. The papers in MH 12 show this concern: they may include, for example, plans for the building of sewage works or municipal bathhouses. Although responsibility for public health was transferred to local authorities in 1894, you may still find papers on the subject.

Possibly the greatest treasures to be found in these volumes, however, are the very rare letters from individual paupers, perhaps making a complaint or bemoaning their fall into pauperism.

ⓘ **Remember**
MH 12 contains few names of individuals admitted to workhouses, but it does include some lists of names of intended emigrants, lunatics and those vaccinated.

If the union ran a workhouse school, there will often be reports from Poor Law inspectors about the quality of tuition and the abilities of the schoolmaster or mistress. A number of neighbouring unions some-times combined to set up a joint school district or a lunatic asylum, especially in the London area. Records of some of these school districts are in the series MH 27. They relate to the administration and control of schools, including the appointment of managers and teaching and nursing staff, inspection of schools, construction and financing of buildings and related medical services.

MH 17 contains similar papers of the sick asylum districts in London and the Metropolitan Asylum Board.

Registers of paid officers (MH 9)

Whitehall had to approve the appointment of staff employed by local unions. Correspondence can be found in MH 12, while registers of people employed by unions are in MH 9. They cover the period between 1837 and 1921, although the vast majority of entries are for the second half of the nineteenth century. The registers are arranged by union. They contain dates of appointments and salary awarded. Reasons for leaving employment are noted, if they were known. Dates of death are also sometimes given, even if the death occurred some time after retirement.

Senior officers are listed in *Shaw's Union Officers' and Local Board of Health Manual*, which was published between 1846 and 1921. Copies of Shaw's are now extremely hard to find, but the PRO holds some.

Applications for employment can often be found in the correspondence in MH 12.

Poor Law inspectors' papers
(MH 12, MH 32)

A team of Poor Law inspectors (before 1848, assistant Poor Law commissioners) was appointed by Whitehall to supervise the work of individual unions. They toured the country reporting on conditions in workhouses and the problems faced by local boards of guardians. From the 1870s specialist inspectors for buildings, infirmaries and schools (including a few women) were increasingly recruited.

The reports of these inspectors can often be found in MH 12, but the main series is MH 32. Here the reports are generally arranged by name of inspector, which can be frustrating if you are trying to track down reports about an individual union.

Local record offices

Collections of Poor Law union records at local record offices are very patchy. Many items were destroyed after workhouses closed, or were pulped as waste paper during the Second World War. As a result, it is not possible to give any clear idea of what might survive for a particular union or workhouse. On the other hand, many of the forms and registers completed by officials contain duplicated information; so if one set of records has been lost, another of a similar type may be equally useful.

A comprehensive list of what records survive for each union can be found in the three volumes of J. Gibson, *Poor Law Union Records*.

Types of record you might find are:

- Minutes of the board of guardians and its various sub-committees. These may contain minutes about troublesome inmates or the apprenticing of individual children. You may occasionally find lists of paupers or, with the appropriate committee papers, lists of pauper children.

- Registers of indoor-relief granted. These records come in various forms, for example registers of admissions and discharges from the workhouse, or printed indoor-relief lists published every six months. There are also creed registers which, from 1876, contain religious and other personal details about paupers.

- Registers of the admission and discharge of vagrants to and from the casual wards.

- Registers of births, baptisms, deaths and burials in the workhouse.

- Registers of children, including admissions to the workhouse school. There may also be registers giving details of the employment of children or where they were boarded out.

- Registers of lunatics in asylums.

- Registers or books of paupers receiving out-relief. There may also be printed outdoor-relief lists showing where every recipient lived and giving the reason why they received support. Also of considerable interest are the application and report books, from 1847, in which details of applications for relief are given.

ⓘ Remember
Records less than 75 years old may not be open if they contain personal information. Local record offices will give information about the position in their area.

OTHER SOURCES

Parliamentary Papers

Parliamentary Papers are also a useful source for tracing pauper ancestors. These records contain much of the information needed by Parliament to conduct its business. It can be hard to track down sets of Parliamentary Papers. Many university libraries will have sets, as should the largest reference libraries. The Parliamentary Archives, at the House of Lords, has a complete set, including those papers which were not published. For many people, however, the most accessible set is the one to be found on microfiche at the PRO in Kew.

More about the PRO's holdings can be found in the leaflet *Parliamentary Papers* (Domestic Records 7) available from the PRO or downloadable from the PRO website (see p. 16).

Fortunately, Parliamentary Papers are well indexed. The index covering 1801–1997 has been published on CD-ROM: a copy is in the PRO library. An alternative is to use the published *General Indexes* which cover the eighteenth and nineteenth and part of the twentieth centuries.

Whether you use the CD-ROM or the *General Indexes*, you will need to grasp the reference system. Each parliamentary paper is assigned a unique reference. For example, the 'Statement for each Month of the Year

1914 of the Number of Paupers Relieved in England and Wales' is Parliamentary Paper 1914.lxix.598.

This reference can be broken down as follows:

- '1914' gives the year of the parliamentary session.

- 'lxix' is the volume in which the paper can be found.

- '598' is the page where the paper begins.

It is very easy to confuse Roman numerals and some volumes have not been paginated, but in general it is a simple system that works well.

There are several types of parliamentary record which might be of use:

Reports and papers of royal commissions and other enquiries

During the nineteenth and twentieth centuries there were a number of royal commissions and other enquiries into the condition of the poor. The two most famous were the royal commissions of 1832–4 and 1905–8. As well as making detailed reports, both commissions ordered that the accompanying evidence be published.

As part of the evidence presented to the commission of 1832, overseers or Poor Law officials were asked to complete a questionnaire about the provision for poor relief in the their parish. Only a fifth of parishes bothered to reply. Disappointed by this return, the commissioners sent a number of assistant commissioners round the country in 1832 and 1833 to report on the position locally. Another fifth of parishes were visited in total.

Although sketchy, this evidence offers a unique view of the lives of poor people in the early 1830s. The commissioners spoke to many labourers, and their views are recorded verbatim in the records. In addition these documents include information about many individual paupers. In Thurgarton, Nottinghamshire, for example, the commissioners visited all the labourers in the village, noting down details of their families and of any savings they might have.

As well as royal commissions, a number of parliamentary committees looked at aspects of the Poor Law or the condition of the poor in general. The evidence presented can give a vivid insight into the life of the paupers. The best known of these enquiries examined conditions in Andover workhouse in 1847.

Annual reports of the Poor Law Commissioners and their successors

The Poor Law Commissioners and their successors presented an annual report to Parliament summarising their work during the previous year. Particularly in the early years, these reports offer another illuminating insight into how the Poor Law operated. It is occasionally possible to find a mention of the cases of individual paupers.

Returns and circulars

These papers contain individual returns made to Parliament, normally at the request of an MP. Often they are just for a single year or a few years. This material includes a return of officials employed at Lady Day, 1848, listing them by union, with details of salary, age and period of service with their present employers. There are also lists (covering part of the 1860s) of paupers who had been in the workhouse for more than five years.

Newspapers

Newspapers are another important – and under-used – resource for studying the Poor Law, particularly the New Poor Law. It is unlikely that individual paupers will be mentioned, however, although the appointment, resignation or dismissal of officials may well be. In local newspapers you are likely to find almost verbatim accounts of the meetings of the boards of guardians, and the occasional account of a visit made by a reporter to the local workhouse. Local newspapers are also likely to feature in great detail debates about the treatment of paupers, especially such minor issues as whether inmates should be allowed beer with their Christmas dinner.

National newspapers also had a keen interest in the Poor Law, particularly in the 1830s and 1840s. *The Times*, for example, led in exposing the Andover Workhouse Scandal. Radical newspapers of the 1830s led the campaign against the introduction of workhouses.

Local record offices and local studies libraries are likely to have newspapers for their areas. The biggest collection of newspapers, however, is held by the:

▼ **British Library Newspaper Library**
Colindale
London NW9 5HE
Telephone: 020 8636 1544
Internet: http://www.bl.uk

The PRO has a microfilm set of *The Times* and an index to it on CD-ROM. The best guide to newspapers is J. Gibson, *Local Newspapers 1750–1920*.

CHARITIES

Charities are another aspect of poor relief of interest to the researcher. They played an important role in looking after the poor. The first charities go back nearly 900 years. One of the earliest that still survives is the Hospital of St Cross in Winchester, founded by Bishop Henri de Blois in 1136 to shelter 'thirteen poor men, feeble and so reduced in strength that they can hardly or with difficulty support themselves without another's aid'. The hospital still looks after old people and provides bread and ale to passing travellers who demand it.

In the seventeenth and eighteenth centuries charities were particularly important in assisting people who for one reason or another did not qualify for support from the Poor Law. However, charitable bodies were not spread equally across England and Wales. They tended to concentrate on the older cathedral cities, which had been prosperous in medieval or Tudor times. The City of London, in particular, had hundreds of charities. They included funds for sermons marking the defeat of the Armada and the failure of the Gunpowder Plot, for the tolling of the bell of St Sepulchre's before executions at Newgate, for the ransoming of Christian captives from Barbary pirates and, most curious of all, for killing ladybirds on Cornhill.

In fact there are two types of charity: endowed and voluntary or subscription. Endowed charities are funds set aside by an individual for a particular purpose, usually in the form of a bequest in a will. Until the nineteenth century charities were largely established by the bequests of rich merchants and others who were charitably minded – or perhaps had half an eye on an easier passage through the pearly gates. These endowed charities (also called parochial) might run almshouses for the elderly and schools for the town's children, or even just provide free coal for the poor on Christmas Day. They had very close connections with the Anglican church, as they were often established by devout churchgoers to benefit poor people of the parish.

As a result, most towns now have an almshouse or two, housing elderly men and women. Many old public and grammar schools were also established as the result of charitable bequests.

Although endowed charities continued to be important in the nineteenth century, they were overshadowed in the public mind by voluntary or subscription charities. These were run by committees and survived largely on donations and subscriptions given by supporters. One of the first was Captain Thomas Coram's Hospital for Foundlings, established in 1739, in Holborn (to which Handel left the rights of *The Messiah*). Tens of thousands of such charities were subsequently formed, ranging from national bodies such as the Royal Society for Prevention of Cruelty to Animals and the Church of England Waifs and Strays Society (now the NCH), to small local funds such as the League of Welldoers and the Sheltering Home for Destitute Children, both in Liverpool.

It is difficult to know how effective these bodies were. Commentators argued that there could be considerable duplication of effort and little coordination between charities in the same field, which could lead to the waste of money and (worst of all) people receiving support to which they were not entitled from several different bodies. The Charity Organisation Society (COS) was formed in 1869 with the aim of reducing this duplication and of training charity workers so that they could better help applicants. However, there was a common perception that it had an unfeeling attitude to the poor: critics suggested that COS stood for 'Cringe Or Starve'.

There was no central control over charities, except during the two world wars, until 1961. As a result, charities proliferated unchecked. In 1999 there were 185,000 charities registered with the Charity Commission. Recent estimates suggest that on the outbreak of war in 1914 there was less than half this number.

Finding the records

It can be very difficult to find records created by charities, partly because there were so many of them and partly because their records have largely been lost.

This is especially true for charities that are no longer in existence. Where they survive, records tend to be at local record offices, although some of the large national charities, such as Barnado's, have their own archives. A list of useful addresses is given below.

Almost all charities produced an annual report. These reports normally included a summary of the year's work, with accounts and lists of committee members and officers, subscribers and donors. Occasionally addresses or other information are included in the subscription list, but normally only name and amount is given. The report might also give details of individuals helped. Frustratingly for family historians, however, they are almost never named.

Very few records of applicants for assistance survive. Where they do, records are normally closed for 75 years to prevent distress to their immediate families, so in practice you might not be able to find very much about individuals after the mid-1920s. Occasionally, reference to individuals can be found in minute books recording the decisions made by the executive committee and any sub-committees.

ⓘ Remember
Most records of charities have been destoryed. Where they survive, they are likely to be at local record offices.

The National Register of Archives should be able to tell you where records for individual charities can be found. Their details can be found on p. 15. Many local studies libraries, whose holdings tend not to be found in the NRA, may also have material, as indeed might the charities themselves if they are still in existence.

Addresses of charities who may have records to assist your research are:

▼ **Age Concern**
National Old People's Welfare Council
1268 London Road
London SW16 4ER

▼ **Barnado's**
Tanners Lane
Barkingside
Ilford
Essex IG6 1DQ

▼ **Children's Society**
Edward Rudolf House
Margery Street
London WC1 OHL

▼ **National Children's Homes – Action for Children**
158 Crawley Road
Roffley
Horsham
Surrey RH12 4EU

▶ **The University of Liverpool Archives
and Special Collections**
PO Box 123
Liverpool L69 3BA

These archives hold the records of a number of charities, especially those that looked after children or encouraged emigration

PRO sources

The PRO is not a particularly good source for anybody interested in charity history or individuals helped by charities. It does, however, have records of a very small number of charities:

- Royal Greenwich Hospital, c.1694–1832 (ADM 65–80)

- League of Mercy, 1898–1947 (MH 11)

- War Refugees' Committee, 1914–19 (MH 8)

- Sarah Cowley and William Clayton Charity for school children in Lancashire, 1758–75 (C 171).

In addition, records relating to a small charity for destitute naval and military officers – the Poor Knights of Windsor – can be found in a number of places, particularly in HO 44. They include applications for appointment, including one from a certain John Bowes to Secretary Hedges in 1705. Bowes wished to be nominated to fill a vacancy as 'he is tired of being a poet' (SP 34/36/126).

References to charities can occasionally be found in Chancery papers. Of particular interest may be the charity briefs in C 48. These are printed papers in the form of a proclamation appealing for charity for the victims of fire and flood and giving licence for collection of alms. They name the victims of the disaster, its time, place and effect, and the total estimated losses; and are endorsed by the churchwardens of the parishes concerned to show the amount of money collected.

The papers of the Charity Commissioners are useful sources, too, particularly their investigations into endowed charities between 1817 and 1850 (in CHAR 2), which often include names of trustees and officials. In CHAR 4 can be found record sheets for registered war charities between 1916 and 1920, which list officers with their addresses.

Material on endowed schools can largely be found in ED 27, ED 43 and ED 49. Investigation into fraudulent charities are in HO 45 and MEPO 3. Records of charities connected with the Queen's Prison between 1842 and 1862 are in PRIS 4. The series includes lists of prisoners who received help.

Charities – further reading

Almost nothing has been published about using charity records for family history. Readers may wish to look at S. Fowler, 'Sweet Charity: Charities and the Family Historian', *Family History Monthly*, June 1999 (no. 45). The best history of British charities is David Owen, *English Philanthropy 1660–1960* (Oxford University Press, 1965), which larger public libraries should have. The PRO library also has a copy.

SEE FOR YOURSELF

Several workhouses are now museums. Ripon Workhouse has recently opened, with restored vagrants' wards from 1877, which show the treatment of paupers in Yorkshire workhouses, and a Victorian 'Hard Times' gallery. The address is:

▼ **Allhallowgate**
   Ripon
   North Yorkshire HG4 1LE
   Telephone: 01765 690799.

The National Trust is restoring Southwell Workhouse, near Nottingham. The Reverend John Beecher built the workhouse in 1824 in order to demonstrate his theories of poor relief. For over 150 years it dominated the local landscape, but by 1997 this nationally important building was under threat of being turned into residential flats. The National Trust stepped in to buy it, however, and started working to secure its long-term future as a monument to the Poor Laws and the poor. It is expected to open at Easter 2002. For more information contact:

▼ **The National Trust**
   East Midlands Regional Office
   Clumber Park Stableyard
   Nr Worksop
   Nottinghamshire S80 3BE
   Telephone: 01909 486411.
   Internet: http://www.nationaltrust.org.uk

GLOSSARY

The Poor Law was a complicated system to operate, and used a number of words and phrases that may not be clear today. Some of the most important terms are defined below:

43rd Elizabeth

The Poor Law Statute of 1601, which established the duty of parishes to maintain their poor.

Gilbert unions

Parishes in towns, or groups of rural parishes, could adopt Gilbert's Act of 1782 in order to build workhouses to house paupers. Until the 1870s, unions were exempt from the 1834 Act.

Guardians

From 1834, officials elected by the rate-payers of a parish to administer the Poor Law locally.

Indoor-relief

Assistance provided within a workhouse.

Oakum

Tarred ship's rope. Unpicking strands of oakum was a task often assigned to female paupers.

Out-relief

Assistance, normally a small pension, provided to an individual at home.

Overseer of the poor

Before 1834, the official elected annually by the ratepayers in the parish to administer the Poor Law locally. There were normally one or two overseers per parish, elected to serve for a year.

Pauper

Person in receipt of assistance from the parish or Poor Law union. To become, and especially to die, a pauper was a matter of great shame amongst all sectors of society.

Poor Law union

Often just called the 'union'. This was the body, under the direction of the board of guardians, responsible for the administration of the Poor Law locally.

Poor rate	Tax levied on ratepayers (people who owned property above a certain value), to pay for the relief of the local poor.
Relieving officer	Official appointed to assess the eligibility of an applicant for admission to the workhouse or to receive out-relief.
Settlement	People were entitled to relief in the parish in which they had right of settlement. Settlement was conferred on individuals either in the parish where they were born or in the parish where they had resided for ten years, or been an apprentice for seven years, or paid the poor rate or rented property.
Settlement examinations	Record of an interview, before two or more magistrates, of a pauper trying to prove right to settlement in a parish.
Vestry	The body administering the Poor Law locally under the Old Poor Law. It derived its name from the room attached to the chancel of a church where the parish authorities originally met. The vestry members were the parish priest, plus churchwardens and leading parishioners, who were either co-opted (in a 'closed' vestry) or elected by the ratepayers (in an 'open' vestry).
Workhouse	The place where paupers were supposed to live under harsh conditions as a deterrent to becoming a burden on the ratepayers.
Workhouse master	The person in charge of running the workhouse. This was a position of considerable responsibility, if low pay.
Workhouse matron	The person, normally the workhouse master's wife, in charge of the female residents. She also oversaw the domestic arrangements of the workhouse.

FURTHER READING

There are a fair number of books on the Poor Law and its operation. Most of the books listed here should be readily available from family history society libraries or your local library. The publications of the Federation of Family History Societies (FFHS) are on sale in the PRO and Society of Genealogists bookshops. There are often articles on aspects of the Poor Law and poverty in Britain in *Family History Monthly, Family Tree Magazine, Practical Family History* and *Ancestors* (published by the Public Record Office), as well as in local and family history society journals. Sets of these magazines and journals are available at the Society of Genealogists, 14 Charterhouse Buildings, Goswell Road, London EC1M 7BA.

I. Anstruther, *The Scandal of the Andover Workhouse* (Alan Sutton, 1984)

A. Cole, *Poor Law Documents before 1834*, 2nd edn (FFHS, 2000)

M.A. Crowther, *The Workhouse System 1834–1929: The History of An English Social Institution* (Batsford, 1981)

J. Foster and J. Shepherd, *British Archives: A Guide to Archive Resources in the United Kingdom,* 3rd edn (Macmillan, 2001)

J. Gibson, *Local Newspapers 1750–1920* (FFHS, 1989)

J. Gibson, *Quarter Sessions Records for Family Historians*, 4th edn (FFHS, 1995)

J. Gibson, C. Rogers and C. Webb, *Poor Law Union Records*, 2nd edn (FFHS, 2000). Vol. 1 covers unions in south-east england and East Anglia; vol. 2 the Midlands and northern England; vol. 3 south-west England, the Marches and Wales; and vol. 4 is a gazetteer of England and Wales showing which parishes were in which union.

B. Hurley, *The Handy Book of Parish Law* (Wiltshire Family History Society, 1995)

N. Longmate, *The Workhouse* (Temple Smith, 1974)

H. Mayhew, *London Labour and the London Poor* (Penguin, 1985)

I. Mortimer (ed.), *Record Repositories in Great Britain,* 11th edn (PRO, 1999)

Public Record Office, *Using Birth, Marriage and Death Records* (PRO, 2000)

Public Record Office, *Using Census Records* (PRO, 2000)

M. E. Rose, *The Relief of Poverty 1834–1914* (Macmillan, 1986)

W.E. Tate, *The Parish Chest* (Phillimore, 1983)

K. Thompson, *Short Guides to Records* (Historical Association, 1997). See especially no. 5, *Guardians' Minute Books*; no. 23, *Quarter Sessions' Order Books*; no. 27, *Overseers' Accounts*; no. 28, *Settlement Papers*; no. 37, *Assistant Poor Law Commissioners' Correspondence*.

Websites

There are two websites devoted to the history of the workhouse and the Poor Law, particularly after 1834:

http://www.workhouses.org.uk

http://www.users.powernet.co.uk/rossbret.index.html

In addition, http://www.genuki.org.uk has a number of useful pages on the Poor Law, as well as links to other sites of interest.